IMPATIENCE

FOR IMMEDIATE RELEASE

A POEM IN 52 PIECES BY SCOTT ZIEHER

EMERGENCY PRESS
NEW YORK

Printed in the United States of America.

Published by Emergency Press
emergencypress.org

Emergency Press is the imprint of the Emergency Collective. A New York non-profit organization, the press is also a member and grant recipient of The Council of Literary Magazines and Presses, and a participant in the Green Press Initiative.

ISBN 978-0-9753623-5-8

9 8 7 6 5 4 3 2 1
First Printing

Cover image:
n/d, found drawing, ink on paper

Author portrait by André Pretorius
2009, watercolor on paper

Book design by Jason Gitlin

Ten percent of the proceeds from this book will be donated to the ALS (Amyotrophic Lateral Sclerosis or Lou Gehrig's Disease) Association in the name of Sally LaVonne Zieher.

FOR

DANNY O'CONNOR

AND

BRYAN TOMASOVICH

"To use this book is a simple matter—Suppose a writer wishes to say a person is a fool but wants a word that is more definite, or more contemptuous, or less blunt. Turning to the index, (see back of book) and to the *F* section, then turning to page 298, he sees the heading(s) STUPIDITY IDIOCY, and then finds the word needed in the list under PERSONS—ape, jay, oaf, yap, dolt, dupe, fool, gawk, booby, chump, crank, dummy, dunce, goose, idiot, moron, ninny, duffer, dotard, donkey, bumpkin, noodle, dullard, lunatic, saphead, imbecile, milksop, numskull, blockhead, greenhorn, ignoramus, simpleton, dunderhead, loggerhead, nincompoop."

GUSTAVUS A. HARTRAMPF, *Hartrampf's Vocabularies*

"And (on the other foot) as fast as a clean man builds up some social consciousness, or the state spends a few million on beautifying the highroads and their borders, some foetid spawn of the pit puts up a 30 foot wooden advertisement of synthetic citronade to defile man's art in road-making and the natural pulchritude of the vegetation."

EZRA POUND, *Guide to Kulchur*

"I like Americans"

EDNA ST. VINCENT MILLAY

INSIDE THIS BOOK!

ALABAMA
ALASKA
ARIZONA
ARKANSAS
CALIFORNIA
CANADA
COLORADO
CONNECTICUT
DELAWARE
DISTRICT OF COLUMBIA
FLORIDA
GEORGIA
HAWAII
IDAHO
ILLINOIS
INDIANA
IOWA
KANSAS
KENTUCKY
LOUISIANA
MAINE
MARYLAND
MASSACHUSETTS
MICHIGAN
MINNESOTA
MISSISSIPPI
MISSOURI
MONTANA
NEBRASKA
NEVADA
NEW HAMPSHIRE
NEW JERSEY
NEW MEXICO
NEW YORK
NORTH CAROLINA
NORTH DAKOTA
OHIO
OKLAHOMA
OREGON
PENNSYLVANIA
PUERTO RICO
RHODE ISLAND
SOUTH CAROLINA
SOUTH DAKOTA
TENNESSEE
TEXAS
UTAH
VERMONT
VIRGINIA
WASHINGTON
WEST VIRGINIA
WISCONSIN
WYOMING

And more!

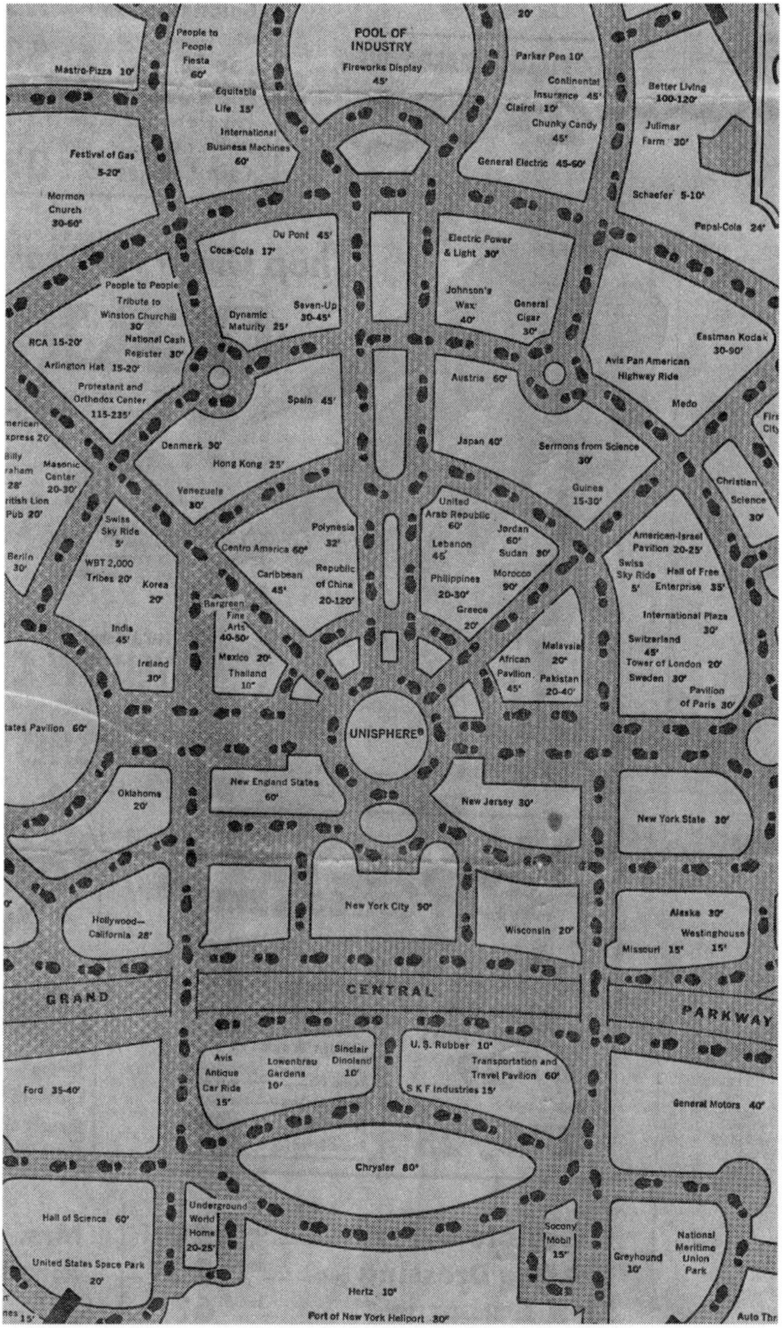
POOL OF INDUSTRY
Fireworks Display 45'
People to People Fiesta 60'
Mastro-Pizza 10'
Equitable Life 15'
International Business Machines 60'
Parker Pen 10'
Continental Insurance 45'
Clairol 10'
Chunky Candy 45'
General Electric 45-60'
Better Living 100-120'
Julimar Farm 30'
Schaefer 5-10'
Pepsi-Cola 24'
Festival of Gas 5-20'
Mormon Church 30-60'
Du Pont 45'
Coca-Cola 17'
Electric Power & Light 30'
Johnson's Wax 40'
General Cigar 30'
People to People Tribute to Winston Churchill 30'
Dynamic Maturity 25'
Seven-Up 30-45'
RCA 15-20'
National Cash Register 30'
Arlington Hat 15-20'
Eastman Kodak 30-90'
Avis Pan American Highway Ride
Protestant and Orthodox Center 115-235'
Spain 45'
Austria 60'
Medo
Denmark 30'
Hong Kong 25'
Japan 40'
Sermons from Science 30'
Masonic Center 20-30'
Venezuela 30'
Guinea 15-30'
Christian Science 30'
United Arab Republic 60'
Polynesia 32'
Jordan 60'
Sudan 30'
Swiss Sky Ride 5'
Centro America 60'
Lebanon 45'
American-Israel Pavilion 20-25'
WBT 2,000 Tribes 20'
Caribbean 45'
Republic of China 20-120'
Philippines 20-30'
Morocco 90'
Swiss Sky Ride 5'
Hall of Free Enterprise 35'
Korea 20'
Greece 20'
Bargreen Fine Arts 40-50'
International Plaza 30'
India 45'
Malaysia 20'
Switzerland 45'
Mexico 20'
African Pavilion 45'
Tower of London 20'
Ireland 30'
Thailand 10'
Pakistan 20-40'
Sweden 30'
Pavilion of Paris 30'
UNISPHERE®
New England States 60'
Oklahoma 20'
New Jersey 30'
New York State 30'
New York City 90'
Hollywood—California 28'
Wisconsin 20'
Alaska 30'
Westinghouse 15'
Missouri 15'
GRAND
CENTRAL
PARKWAY
Avis Antique Car Ride 15'
Lowenbrau Gardens 10'
Sinclair Dinoland 10'
U. S. Rubber 10'
Transportation and Travel Pavilion 60'
S K F Industries 15'
Ford 35-40'
General Motors 40'
Chrysler 60'
Underground World Home 20-25'
Socony Mobil 15'
Hall of Science 60'
United States Space Park 20'
Greyhound 10'
National Maritime Union Park
Hertz 10'
Port of New York Heliport 30'

(FOR IMMEDIATE RELEASE)

A POEM (IN FIFTY-TWO PIECES)

FIRST DRAFT OF A PREFACE

Hereby a found song (and every chorus equals whole the knavery of an un-shuffled deck)—a second breath from the lucky long what bellows its baker's dozen. Note for the Macaronicon ensconced and cooped at still antique Manhatta—swing not that brittle basket now. Be the first (instead) on your social register and hurry to sign up for the spring term's course on free verse interludes in the Modern Age administered by the guy at the delicatessen who wears his checkered scarf so snug. (Or a multi-fractured portrait of your stationary ad-copy man's exuberant voices gone—daft like an avenue yes man after much travailing.) We sell attractive, distinctive, colorful, washable displays in process oil, show cards, price cards, glass, metal, cloth, wood, cardboard, and paper signs, motion displays, felt pennants, lamp shades, bakelite signs, real estate signs, decorative novelties, tire cover printing, fabric novelties, and all flat surfaces regardless of thickness. We toil. We never nod to anxiety. We filter the silt. We are Alaskan dogs on undershirts—not funny. We are small men in skull-caps even when we are women. Note for a preface—endgames are optional at the crime scene where we smoke our rather more surreptitious cigarettes. How hangs the lonely man's axe? High. We infuse the bones with ink and drain until tender. We are half again how much we weighed upon departure (in the parlance of cheese manufacturers universified). Note for a holy preface—we are a serious set of canoodlers for you. Note for a preface—from the mixed-up desk of a traveling plumbing salesman's daydreamt wanderlusts (mainly from within the amygdale, that almond-shaped mass of mediocre matter in each hemisphere of the brain which governs feelings of aggression). Note for a preface—no extreme kerning, no more widowed lines. How turns this racer's inside wheel? Wide. Note toward a preface—no apologies for snapshots of actual play in the sharp and darting scrimmage, halfback flâneur behind a lunching mid-fielder's idle interference and the team preparing again their long wishbone. Large size milk wagon note for a preface (a walking rain of nationwide phrases)—all of these and more!

SECOND DRAFT OF A PREFACE

Note for a preface—achieve overall betterment among your clientele—notice their whimsy smirks and battleship-tin-hammered resolve. And another note for a preface—200 pieces of Turkey Red Damask, exceedingly scarce, with full line of wool and Eiderdown tam o' Shanters. (See once more the crime scene where we smoke our rather more surreptitious cigarettes.) And note for a preface—the stations of impatiens. Several hundred self-portraits were found yesterday in an unidentified attic on the hill-cusp between the Benjamin Franklin and Alexander Hamilton sections of town, each water-marked Workmen's Standard Time Book Weekly and full of pot roast language. Memo-random for a preface—we met when the snow was shoulder high and the air was warm enough to melt it all. We rolled one up and threw it off the bridge. One can't say enough about certain jazz music. Especially the very early works that were ever-so-delicately reconstructed from the fragments left behind in crawlspaces above fireplaces on Jack Sharkey Road through the picturesque and delicate purlieus of Stanley, Sterling, Gladstone, Adams and New England, North Dakota (amid the whistling fire baptized windows admixed with supervisor's encouragement language). Note for a preface—back of comic book page language. Pile Fabric Primer language. Wrench and hammer language. Hot dog napkin deliveryman language (an outskirt language). Note for a preface—usurp same for poesy.

THIRD DRAFT OF A PREFACE

All articles in this catalog are guaranteed to give the service you deserve and have a right to expect if our directions for use are carefully followed. Step right up and don't be phony, call it cheese and macaroni! Meine kleine Bahnhofhallenbüchlein Aktendeckelkarton. This gum protects the gauze of penny dreadful cardboard dossier covers and a wonderful strength is given by way of exceptional strain in testing for other covers that will also fit sifting machines, sieve bolters, round reels and hexagons. Prompt shipments to all points top and bottom. Pitch language, manual language, pamphlet language, lingo for phonography teachers, tongue for ambulance mechanics, encyclicals for fire engine graveyard keepers, night language for lingerie box makers, ephemera for men, jetsam for girls, the documents of ukulele manufacturers and wildcat Pontiac hubcap salesmen, not to mention menu adverbs, haberdasher's adjectives, fountain pen hospital repairmen's argot, the fine art of epistolary pencils (note for a preface with handshakes) and another note for a preface with nods to a man by name of the Kansas City business-poet Tom King Baker and his now defunct $326,000,000 turnpike language. Furthermore, the language of fishermen hunting and bowlers playing basketball (now there's some sugar in that slang for sure) in addition to the complete drawings, the entire Irv (each Patchen, each Pound, each Bunting, Wheelwright, Fearing and all three Vladimirs), that singular ad-copy man in a smudge colored suit. The derrick's up and trucks are cash—the envelope in front of you carries our coveted stash.

PASSION WAXES

Looking for something fun this coming summer? Enjoy Boys Glee! Set your cunning sails on the elastic latitudes, bulging parallels and fugal graticules of Gotham-on-Hudson—these north-eastern shores along our great nation of yore. Set those sun-speckled sights on our super-fast beyond, wherein you'll witness scenes considering broad human interest including the invention of our typewriter and nine hints for a better spice cabinet-full of scribbles, right here—where Dutch Street dies and the Maiden lumbers under, where Fletcher barely butts the wall of Water. Glance up from your workaday, silly! Watch your bellhop spit cherry pits into the palm of his hand. Inhale the wild-eyed wind—inherit the arrogant, perilous, un-swallowed city via Elbert Hubbard and thereby Wallace Nutting too. Tally every hotcake for Pete's famous creeping sake. This work will show you the long and wordy, pedestrian way to wind-rifting advances and raking light, the backward stances of the academy against youthful bewilderment in a clean white shirt. Fanfares for as far south as Alabama and the ham-handed parade in a downward glance facing north as the fifth floor blooms to blinding. Looking for something stupid this hyperactive holiday? Well you've come again to the right, square damnable place.

INDIANAPOLIS THE METROPOLIS

Willkommen Alles and Huzzah from the Hinterlands—the extravaganza you've long awaited and always expected would never arrive has landed on three feet at last, right here in Indiana! And such a circus it is—incorporating folk humors and long silences, glorious hues akin to blue, brief sirens and the hilarity of a screeching, nut-crunching punctuation—fully unhinged from their shaky collective sheaves. All are indeed welcome herein except those who chew their bubble-gum-cud out loud. A veritably involuntary manslaughter for certain, rally-cries for shame, and sea-doped barracudas for joy—you can hack your fondest memories into gigantic fjords of solid ice to boot! Come down on Monday, remove paw from pocket, come down on Tuesday—we simply don't care when you come! Just be there and wear your best bells, for the extravaganza you've long awaited and always expected would never arrive has landed on all three feet in the snow-fence state at last.

ALOHA FROM IDAHO

Need to get down and dirty? Ferret out your concierge! He's wearing a bright green vest coat and a velvet neck tie. Actually, strike that—grab yourself an ink-pen, an extremely tall sleeve of ice-cold Dry Sack, a pair of dice and a basket of optimistic snack foods. Quiet your most lackadaisical of tongues! Pass the pour-able mustard, we thirst! Who said the uppermost northwest doesn't know how tight trousers function of a dark and dreary Sunday morning? Not this inheritor of the grape. Not this foreign sun from the cheese castle. Not these! Who turned down the music? Who'll bid his every warrant? We do dare say get your skinny one back to position and squat with your shotgun aimed at the target and fire on the Patron Saint of Pontiacs—his ass in a very old masterpiece.

CHICAGO LOUSY WITH POETS

It took more than one millennia to invent a horse for meat and we just named it—*Beef and Brandy.* Almost everybody always does sidle a flabby, avuncular backside into town via the 3:00 Hiawatha Southerly out of Joliet (and prepares to drink a liquid comestible by name of Sterling). All 26 chairs are full of your brother-in-law's finest slack style, and these folks know how to eat the food they're served amid the pipe smoke. Man by name of Uhle urges his regular bunch (up by the smoke shop) *not* to memorize the perfect blend, but mix, instead, fresh tobaccos on a regularly rotating basis so as to always be on the prowl for that most righteous new combination (keeps a body guessing). You're a long snake in the cooling reeds and medium grasses. Archways draped with Northerns, muskellunges—potted plants from Cuba and this is a steakhouse! Labeled so by the windiest nook in the oldest town we know between here and Missouri. Have you ever seen a product move so smoothly? We didn't think so Madame. Ask to see her keychain. Ask to see her shiniest breastplate.

WORLD PREPARATORY TELEGRAM

By the Teeny Weenie Canteen just but seven footprints to Roosevelt Avenue Division of Long Island Railroad & House of Good Taste & Singer Bowl Maryland Express & West Virginia room pillar, Illinois recognizance, New Mexico neverlandish, Hollywood (Anger) California & porridge of Oklahoma, this whole world's fairest of the fair is among the most fabulous ever, stop! Also United States of America's Round Pavilion, stop. Here, young girls spoon blueberry flummery in smiling heapfuls. More fun than a truck! Ireland & India all 200 tribes & Swiss Sky Ride Korea & Masonic Center within the American Express kiosk & British Lion Pub where warm beer does flow evenly & steady-handed. Here, young girls in jacket dresses inquire about animals around the Question House. Arlington Hats & Protestant & Orthodox Center National Typesetter Cash Register & the People to People Tribute again with long, lazy Swedish Sky Rides, Gotthold Ephraim Lessing not withstanding, the libraries of Leipzig (all the rage here) stop.

HOW TO FLIP A BARGAIN INTO A BEAUTY

Raucous, wily, winterized, jackbooted thieves run from the windswept storm ravaged Des Moines right-of-ways to the acne of Ohio with a grimace. Our fast-acting cream wipes away the future two days in advance of the most recent past. Stop tomorrow's pimples yesterday! Like her mid-sized city sisters, the farmer's wife who buys a new one-minute-automatic finds a box of all new stuff inside. Dad knows it pays to take the advice of many experts all in one, rolled together like a wonder fry fire king. Not many others put stuff inside. This instant mix sends out strong meat signals men can't resist. How should he go about covering the seats of his chrome chairs in plastic? Simple! Just follow the fourteen steps in order, and *voila*, look here, the task is fast. What a powerful liver herein. The liver is the cock's comb. These perpetual blemishes shy away from sharing. They run thick below the rooftops here and don't give a smear for your heart-aches no matter how droopy and doe-eyed you make your proposal.

WINTRY LODGE ON A WHITE MOUNTAIN

Wine and dine and after the hunt we call the dogs together around the footstool and all manner of sot-scape, have a draught, inhalations most robust. Our guns are clean as whistles, our whistles are slightly wet. We've thanked our commodious hostess. The dogs take taboo sleep. Their fog-headed, gum-rheumy blear-eyes clammed over as if they'd slept for days or so already. We laughed through the black and pink proceedings. The telephone prattled in its cradle severally. The typewriter was manhandled with many absent-minded and suspensive smacks and did come full-swing, full-throttle homeward as a well-heeled moth of rusty colors and chalky complexion alights on the stag's nostrils only to follow its destiny and path pre-ordained to find cashmere near (and venison leather). No food is truly blue, except our cheese and the whole berry family, plump as thumbs. And those were some damn fine fruit platters, greasy as the sun shines high. Are you still there whiling away among the hunters newly returned with flasks and pelts of hare past the gleaners and reapers, toward the inn which isn't open? The moon empties out gladsome, the village is well and the hut's not far from here either. A soft group of apes is a shrewdness. Jaw muscles bristle over gristle. Gentler specimens otherwise asleep at their plates, ties wiped with sauces. Poor, tired dogs, all.

COLUMNS BY A CALM POOL

It pays to feed. We're not but half a day away from the rolling hills of Delaware. Wander among the hanging glass. Grip lightly the railings upward. We saw the alderman gargle—*add a comma before tree crotch.* We want challenging color problems. Does your hair need a doctor? Mister Tino is now associated with us. It pays to feed real muscle meats and offal with sixteen pounds of water, milk and blood (for mixing liquids). Come down and spend some of that old-time city scrip! We pamper clients who dread that dyed look with dry-to-brittle whisker-locks. What with the brew-ha-ha and clamber at the hand-me-down-shop. When meat is short go quarter fish and quarter horse-meat or rabbit-meat with bone. Liquid for mixing is scarce. The gentleman from Selma says our silver pelts fetched over one hundred squares on the open market. The horse on Pastor Zell's buggy is named Easy.

PROPOSAL FOR A FOURTH AVENUE KIOSK

Short pink and powder-baby-bottom blue-eggshell neon sign spins—anamorphoses! Hidden to all without mirrors (ideal spot—next to a shop that sells mirrors). Postcards avail, as well as newspapers and envelopes. Short films on Nijinsky, Chaney and Kid Chocolate. Soda jerk for your convenience—all flavors, wanderlusters. Three stools. Tiny stage behind a spinning display of antique tablets for penmanship and cartes de visite manifestoes, hotel billhead, and pennants celebrating the epoch of the golden wolf. Sunshine avail in excelsis during daytime. Stools added under umbrellas at crepuscular clemencies. Steins of local beer avail. Trumpet performances nightly and twice on Sunday (Matinee at Noon).

THE SMALLEST

The nation's most diminutive entity proudly presents the inaugural issue of our back-pocket-shaped hand-manual and just in time for the County Haberdasher's Board of Directors Tri-Annual Shareholder's Meeting. Drop down your triangles and shavers, your awls and punches and lathes, ladies, our end-all cyclopedia and quick reference guide will be in your willing palms by weekend's end. The quick reference index is conveniently priced at no charge to you (our valued and courteous clientele) and can be found on display everywhere your Oldsmobile motor car can caterwaul you. Don't miss Best Friday's festivities and join our top-notch day jobbers, our blue-chip bespoke workers, and our Chief Financial Generalissimos around the snack platters disingenuously provided by Norma's Mom, fulsome and stable after her stroke. See you Sunday.

CALIFORNIA WELCOMES YOU!

Everywhere north and west of Nevada opens up grand, oak doorways to this country of best things. Here you may escape winter cold with wide avenues and pepper trees, layer after layer below hillside poppies aflame in riotous colors. Stop having middle of the mediocre road experiences! Become a palm tree! Enjoy every morning! Become a fish taco! Rid yourself of rickets—join the team around a piping hot dish of medium rare sweetbreads. Get eaten! Our lady of the awkward interlude needs a good night's sleep among the tree dots and hill spots of a small red star between downtowns. And here, too, the man of business, seeking new fields of endeavor and happy-trousered weeks can heartily inhale warm meals served from anywhere east of Georgia (en route to Nebraska) in observation cars bearing names related to the conquest's hardy barking. These include the Frank & Musso, the Early Hollis Frampton and the Salon Car named for Canadian Deanna Durbin. Drawing room segmentations contain ten sections and rear flyaway. In this cozy corner you shall find modish letterhead and clever books. There are numerous ground-glass lights in both ceiling and sides. The colors, they don't jangle. Sleek schemes are used. The scene screams past. This is beatitude embodied—today no really high-class train is considered completely equipped without a car of this description—skillful barbers will hair-cut you, singe you, shave and shampoo you, to be availed of when most convenient. This is Winslow, Oklahoma passing fast—the expense is trifling. In unusual perusals you can walk back and forth from coast to coast without repeating yourself.

A GLORY OF MAUDLIN WATER

We've been wondering where in hell you were. For ourselves, we've been tucked under snifters—we've been mimicking the grille-work and medley through muddy windows—we've surmised the tree's line in the rain that reeks with cheaper varieties. Pretty much anything what moves down here has been killed, fried-up and eaten. Thirsty? Weakest milk. Those were cool pockets marbled into blasts as hot as oven brick. Then red earth and fell trees on the street. Orion's skinny ass is always there. One blames his darker, interior music, and then his wickedest arm's intentions. All the way to Ponce de Leon he hangs with his long sword shining in the morning. Wicked jays peck the breeze-angered grass. And this morning it's goodbye Messers Bonaparte and Brando and so long brief Louisiana. Ladies and Gentleman Miss Gonzalez Jambalaya! It is night and you are all dust behind us. Good night in deed and punishment.

WHAT RESTED ON THE SHELF

Here's newfangled Wenatchee Washington! The grass is spider high. Note the genuflection of sky above a switchback stream. Put on your waders and get ready to cast for steelhead circa Philip Freneau and (you can believe it!) these fish never die. So take these decrees from the better of your born-again brotherhood. Rally cries decorate byways and waysides. Who drives the truck? The younger boy above us who knows how his needle is thread in harder times. Who strikes salmon among the garden greens? Younger boys recoiling from the scop's noodling intimacy (that's who). They prefer a primer of earliest furniture rimes, harrowing tales from garret-styled farmhouses (these are his shelves and nobody messes with the mud of my boy). So spread the gamp and fish. Pass the waxy boxes. Pass their corners full of diamond dust and others with skeletons and guts. The monkey fish is rather red and stupid.

BUCKMINSTER EMPTY

Sad, what blessings befall our sorry state, wishing for the up-shown throne. Wishes are application-specific fasteners and screw them tight my fine standing and tempestuous patriots—we need as much strength as we can muster now. Sextant! Look to our fore-sisters! A pearl clasp once caught in the fingers of an opera-loving pawnbroker's wife. Each of us looks on mute while the dome proves every dame dumb. The champion watches over while we lose. This victory is scarce to cherish. A war doll badly balding doesn't know how dastardly our ratio of tarnation—high and steady, high and rising rapidly, very high and falling slowly, high and falling slowly, high and falling rapidly—forecasting is fun and losing can be hilarious for the winner!

THE DIAPER PEOPLE

Explore cozy Florida—the land where people live forever but their houses don't. All hail the wailing babies of automatically deep neglect, these who drip with mucous, watch them each—a dim child aspirating peanuts while the brighter bulb spits up her purple juice. Pops is now sound and deep atop his quarterly earnings. Mother's reading so as to memorize acupuncture meridians. Uncertain sunshine drifts unbroken upon departure near the stationhouse at the slippery tarmac (that is also ticklish). People die regularly and other people suffer not the while. Each exhale conspiracy, *breathing together,* kneeling together and believing together until the master shows them each something safer than blowing on the fire together. This slow denominator, life—kiss it if you wish, grilled to perfection, with butter—just a little gift for the seamstress in all of us. Licensed Victualers Association cannot be responsible for transfers or rebates and will not accept returns. Sound like a bit of heaven on earth? Then sign up for the retreat to watery Camp Weed (twenty double rooms have been blocked). Kick back along our lapping shore (exploring came the wanderers once). Watch a dollar turn (quick) to a nickel. Dawdle and evaporate! This includes five meals. Retreat and reflect! Watch disappointment blossom like a tiger lily or envelopes of smoke in the chapel.

TELEGRAM IN LIEU OF A BOARD OF DIRECTORS MEETING

Gentle perusal of wares at Bargreen Fine Arts (immaculately controlled dry-point portraits of Gutzon Borglum & Frederic Auguste Bartholdi, tastefully framed {just off center} in a matching pair of uncommonly pristine Dutch Ripple frames) & Mexico's Dead Day of beer is near in the opaque recollection of a thicker heat, stop. Rococo Thailand & Baroque New England States & Brew Moore's Unisphere & New York City (as always) & Yon Olden Homestead Wisconsin (stops here the dollar) toward glorious, runny New Jersey. (Get off at Secaucus Station, retrace the Hotel Ansonia & Parsippany Hawk & Mount Hope & Dover {overcast} with darker eyes at Net Cong's ice-rock, Mount Olive's roadside attractions, outcrops & formations. Oh Dunmoore to Throop in the pouring torrents! Oh Lackawanna Coal Mine Tour & falling rocks & falling rocks & roadside mountain slopes! Oh southerly-running deltas!) Caribbean & Centro-Amerigo Polynesia & effervescent Republic of China, gonad Hong Kong & airplane Venezuela, gilt Denmark & Spanish Dynamic Maturity, stop. National Cash register again of course & Dupont & Coca-Cola. Rolling through the hilly mnemonics of Queens County. Electric Power Light & Johnson's Wax General Cigar & Austria pants, Japan pants & United Arab Republic culottes & Jordan toilet water, torrid Lebanon, Sudan handkerchiefs, Morocco recollection in a slim dust-jacket, Greece having an arch armature of charm, Pilipino brass & the African Pavilion, Brick of Malaysia, Pakistan piquant & New Jersey again for we can't forget to allow for eating time. Several tumescent tomatoes & Bermuda onions (mere pennies on the barrel). Sawbuck on beer for the boys & this here is one heck of a hayride.

THE STONING OF DUMBSHOWMEN

Sloppy sots—watch them sleep and witness parabolic curvatures from down-east to Detroit all along the withering riversides. Slow church ahead, slow thickly settled. Slow trampoline by the train tracks and river beds. Slow for sale. Don't know what amen means? Whole Pennsylvanias of pipe! Simmer the black and blue inks as you would a chicken, live life like a budgie on a glass of milk. They're beautiful, easy to train, inexpensive, clean and they can be taught to talk and not just a word or two, either, but entire sentences! A moody zone, when Thursday seems like Sunday. This bruise, that noose. The hammer is still well-struck and hard on the fallen anvil, porous as balsa. The sweaty fist and grimy wrist, the harmonies and unexpurgated hammer-rhythms—we all raise hell once in awhile. Watch us on our booze-weary ways with torsion just as crooked (this was at Topeka). We were upwards of the northern line and somewhere right in the middle of the route to Shakopee, Deephaven and Independence, Minnesota (respectively)—we wobbled through the train entire. (And the land-locked surfer's fellowship of Oklahoma assured us we were members of the tribe, a sorry set of very saddened stooges in summertime. One of us was a box guitar player.) Some long hours we wobbled no doubt with our seven dollars left and wanted to switch to beer anyway. Afterward and sadly we sent the young box guitar player back to his paces. He was heard of once, abed in Wall, not far from the pharmacy (bleach and boxcars) his ambidexterity torn from its tendons.

TELEGRAM IN LIEU OF A SECOND BOARD OF DIRECTORS MEETING

Farmlands stand with hanks of cheese loaf and another look at the scalding skirt with a heart just as big as a mango. The curds are curious like Anchorage Anchovies—let's have both at once for lunch, oh howdy & hail all you hungry tummy tamers! Westinghouse & Missouri's downtown airport & Minnesota Bourbon Street Vatican & Belgian Village Trifecta—Christian Science, First National City Bank & Garden of Meditation over cups of coffee. Avis Pan American Highway ride rife with several refrigerators full of Kodachrome. Coca Cola & (yum) Schaefer. (About face to touch her satin costume.) For Better Living trust Julimar Farms (have a grapefruit) & browse the *Garden Center 1944* portfolio of Our Maestro of Utopia steeped in Mary Baker's entrancing thrums, hiding diligent behind this very curtain. General Electric Chunky Candy Clairol Continental Insurance Parker Pen Scott Paper & an ice cold can of Rheingold with Boy Scout Troop Admiralty (a topside stop like a gymnastic jamboree for toddlers). Double sawbuck on beer for the boys as we learn with the curve of a quiver. Non-stop greetings from our Fair World!

CHOOSING THE YOUNGSTER

Ozark Ripley says there's been a lot written on the subject of choosing, but it is of little inport to the amateur who wishes to select and master a bitch-dog for his own sport-shooting, or, if she has the nature and peculiar ability, later to make the bitch-dog a contender in the field and fury. Very little can be told of the hump-alpha-female-youngster-romping in prior advance, though some wayward men reputed to be versed in lore convey the deep impression that they are capable of telling instantly what one among a litter of fracas-happy puppies will later make the best bitch of the lot, or else as the useless adjunct of a tired retirement in housewifery or dog-husbandry or man-battle and distaff sorcery—divorcery. Now, someone attract attention with your own commotion so as to get the noted butcher out to dress the fowl and everybody, let's eat!

LOCALS RECONFIGURE PROSPECT TOWER

The world's hungriest academic spelunkers converged in disagreement today among the sassy transparencies of Ravenswood, West Virginia. An angry crew of locals reconfigured the ancient sticks of ye old prospect tower on the village brown—their point was taken as a surlier band of nearby neighbors, numbering in the teens, took up kindling from as many porches as they could locate in silent protest, symbolically reconstructing the ivory-minded model of their long-haired, early-bearded philosophical treatises. *Why paint the house?* they were heard to cry. *Let it breathe!* they said. *Why dig deep when you can climb high? Let oneself fly!* it seems they were muttering. So they set the house on fire. Though the battle played through without incident out of doors, in of doors was another matter, as one big builder (who escaped unscathed) accidentally slapped down a matronly challenger who was sorry for something purple such as this. An oily woolen sweater saved the demurring lady who kicked her cake away, icy as a sniper, falling softly on pillow knit. The tower was soon dismantled by the volunteer fire corps lately summoned by siren. None were dead but the commune's cat, Santa, was reported missing, last seen fleeing the scene diagonally through the maple trees above Wadsworth Avenue.

AT HOME (WITH SNAPS OF PINK)

Fulsome frog pond! Arrogant dragonflies two! The hills are timid to the boot, the yellow dog's yawp and the owl's hoot. Loud colors profess to work like a sea—small tsunamis of encouragement! Handsome floodtides! Swaths of silk and medium royal mountains tally through the oxlips west of Greenwich Mean. Aggravations bloom like rosehips, like monkey pox gone golly far. Caterwauls of limey rime perform, like octopi snacking on wing-nuts. The porous border isn't a fiction but still has phantasmagoria in its foam. Get thee to a library. See those flowers there? See them training for the light. See heat beckon and slow. See the light add up to a hand-picked hailing.

NOT VERMONT

Independence on the fourth of goddamned July and you can hear a hearse through the trees—can hear the horses (acres away) from the last grass of not so much as Verde Monte, as early summer pastorals of the torrid wall before the spruce before the clouds before a clank of barns in red and a warped tangle of metal waste, refuse from a former farm perhaps. There are two types of folks in the world—those who would shoo a hornet and compete till the hornet might go away or secondly, those that would kill a hornet outright. New Hampshire is over the border. Sooner recovered, the clouds dash north. Across these parcels, across yonder mountain's grave crest and valley breasted, ranger bees and mint-colored trees and trees and trees in the pestering depths. And there are ripples of wind across the slanting pasture and the yellow house, crepuscule crisp as new clouds appear—tall and proud from the brain of sky. But sun shines all the time. The sun is always shining. The other barn is gracious brown. The mountain dilates evenly under a shifting wind on buried branches—fully deciduous applause. Sere leaves but full of life, even from a distance.

PHILOSOPHY FOR COMFORTABLE LIVING

Visit the smallest human appointments in history—just one tiny room! His gigantic tub is your diminutive sink. Underneath his tub is the master's bedroom, the rug his grand veranda. A slightest trickle warms his night, your tubes. A bath-tub is his pool, immaculacy in grandiloquence. There can be no argument with water. His stepstool is a dictionary. The wall's a mural—*The Triumph of Kaleidoscopes* and the mural's a riff on *The Demise of a Chinese Game.* He uses the bath-mat for a nap upon radical occasion. Scaffolds hang from grout-hooks and lightly he treads on these, chalking up tile with candle-soot, drawings of tow-headed, flaxen-cap doxies off the farm—girls with waves of healthy wheat hair, drawn smaller and smaller, in a blend of bubbles which once were drifting through the window pane or down the gargling drain.

CERTIFICATE OF AUTHENTICITY

All hail Waukesha Wisconsin Night as Chicago Faucet's Northern Division proudly announces its Annual Regional Salesman's Awards. Light snacks will be offered, along with beer heartily provided by Foxhead and Gettelman and a midnight sitting of Vienna Sausages, cheese fondue, French onion soup, boiled cod, candied yams and a barrel of newly unearthed, deeply buried Tawny for afterward. This year's recipient, Norman Gilbert, whose porcelain sink and brass knob roadwork (combined with sale volume from Davenport to Pardeeville and back again) qualifies him as the embodiment of the Chicago Faucet motto of matter versus manner. Norm receives the award in his finest corduroy suit of deepest virid. Like mantel and molten are also skin and skeleton, he is a static iron filing magnet and his handsome certificate will be hereby granted on Tuesday's foxing Aurucana shell paper. Each regionaire will receive a handsome door-prize for attending. No smoking in the garden this afternoon due to the egg hunt. High volt Chicago Faucet sweater vests are still available for $12.00 in Human Resources. See Verne or Nancy. Due to the weekend's nest flood over by the warehouse, next Friday's Spaghetti Dinner has been rescheduled for the previous Monday at Noon.

HANGOVER CURE FOR MEN

Felix Liquor Rex— signing on with you and a new item from the room service staff at Hotel Allerton Annex. Yes, the King of Happy Juice reminds you to insure a clear head for that morning householder's conference with an Annex Late-Night Sandwich Special—the *Green Bay Greedy Belly*—heaped high and seething with melted heartland American cheese layered between electrifying slivers from our gigantic shank of home-made bologna. Make your last meal a tasty one for sure! Supper side dish options include Uncle Glen salad, with frozen peas and carrots in a tempting mayo-toss. All mayonnaise, all the time. Or try our Western Omelet Sandwich with coleslaw. Teach your stomach the ultimate lesson. Each sandwich comes with a Kosher Dill Kenosha pickle. Call Russ at reception to order now and he'll bring a yellow paper receipt with proof of purchase! Collect a dozen of these and win a free night's stay in the Secretary's Suite. Only midnight or later on weeknights and not available at our Las Vegas location.

THE CORRESPONDENT'S CORRESPONDENCE

Tired of interloping between the blanket and the desk lamp? Had enough of the fragile mooring snapping fast as noon? Weary of the local plumber's jackboots? Smeared you say? Well watch the mail sail into its dented box complete with familiar chamber-tunes gently scraping the ear on each side of your head-dress. Such gear came cheap from far-away where there is no word for whatsoever of an evening elsewhere deemed a boring morning's split hair. And the whimper of nickelodeons regularly from stairwells. Though the world can refer to this day as early summer and the sky can call it later spring, the due course of time has been chill as a tin whistle this April, lately. So draw. Listen to the pins hit and touch and spawn and recollect a hootenanny long since past. Blind Robins are a pair of pennies each. It got cold quick-like. Yesterday was raining sheets of the shit. Memories are not always stained-glass, but sometimes look like heavy rain disintegrating on a Pasadena subpoena. See tree with squirrel, see nut-fellow racing to his burial place.

GRAMMATICA IOWA

A new kind of prickly fun, a peculiar pleasure (not only pleasing but fashionable)—and a truly great game. Don't delay the delight of playing it, hurry to ask your dealer, beg, borrow or buy Iowa and just be sure to play Iowa! (Vanilla malt) cousin Milt works hard and says it plain—*it is a brilliant game of extraordinary and unfathomable fascination.* Easily learnt and differing widely from any other easily learnt endeavors, this battle-like game presents innumerable combinations of perplexing problems—an original type each time. Its real delight will come, however, when a dutiful and industrious, an eager and exaggeratedly passionate, four-handed, many-parted-player is sufficiently advanced to use profound adroitness and sweet strategy in ultra-combat. Engage in violently rewarding maneuvers with only occasional yawps of botheration from truly extreme crises skipping off the damnable leaning lips of some cock-eyed left-tenant or posh corporal or tricked-out ensign or such. From Joop to Waterloo—halloo ballyhoo! Go to! Sally forth, cocksure Iowa players, proceed!

AUTHORIZATION TO DESTROY INVENTORY

Just out of smithereens via Standard Motel en route to Bellflower Boulevard, in California but stuck here in Utah for the moment and by the by—looking for Thrifties do you know them? Have here the significant paperwork to make haste in disposing of the remaining documentation from the incident in the hills off Richfield. Sometimes the *west* sounds like a cure and other times like a curse, where the *goaded* byway waxes mad. There's a key pattern around this building, giving it an aura of impenetrability and also inescapability if you follow. Shy and unpracticed in *the strife of phrase*. God forbid. So far this unburdened morning we haven't put our precious little still-life into anybody else's incapable hands, but the day is fresh and young. Our fate will depend on the sobriety, sanity, skill and sportsmanship of a great many other men, women, and even children who will turn out of their driveways this morning. The Boston-like sportsmanship of other men like Three-Martini Marlowe, Hot-Rod Harry, Road-Hog Roger, Slow-Poke Percival and good, old Napoleon Norbert. Each of them will hold in *his* hands the power of a hundred horses and, at the touch of a toe, will command the velocity of a rogue wave toward a lighter craft (or tiny island). As we don't get behind the storm-tossed wheel, it will be small comfort to recall an item in the gory morning paper—civilian leaders had been called, the item said, for a conference to do something about the reckless people who drive down thunder-wracked Route Seven on their way to grunt-work at the brassiere factory or to deep blue movie picture numbness. Sometimes we think we might walk. But we won't, any more than you will.

THE WRECK OF BIG VALLEY

Dateline—Bering Sea, out of Kodiak, Alaska. Five were lost this last fishery. Boats heave and dive in rough weather, large waves break over the weaving gunwales, and the wooden deck planking often ices over. They skipped sleep to launch and haul, plundered to the rhythms, one with mechanism around his neck, another with marvelous appointments and a third from Uruguay. All were shoulder-men. One was found. None were cautious. Cherish such a life as those. Hunt the long blue map of waters for a tiny red star. This was the iron meter mooring piece just above the acoustic release. Wagging working grounds delay the sailing. So they delay their deployment. If only delay were again the worry. Starboard rolling, splashes of thrashing and flash, frantically raked, to perish elsewhere, further west and north and long and cold and wave and porous, deliquescent and excurrent.

TELEGRAM STEADS A FINAL BOARD OF DIRECTORS MEETING

Rotunda at the Pool of Industry, spy-port at American & Russian Orthodox Sino-Amerigo Churches, Gate Seven affords easy exit. Tall Gals Dress Magic—you will find this bilious Blouson sheath irresistible & you will be too, when you wear it, rayon acetate blue or pink sizes ten through twelve only. Check Bell Telephone. Check Traveler's Hall of Education & People to People Fiesta, Equitable Life with International Business Machines. Check Formica & Pavilion of American Interiors. Simmons offers thirty plus minutes nap time on your own enjoyable stroll, so be sure to stop on by—try Oregon. Try Maestro Pizza. Try Atometric Hospital & mail postcards at United States Post Office Exhibit. Mormon Church Festival of Gas. Another House of Good Taste. Glory be & gather round! Signing off with Beefeater, neat, yeoman of Old High German Beefeater, neat indeed. Kick our loafers to the sofa, hand-over the time-table & confirm the first train to Irvington in the morning, stop. As ever, more soon.

THE MONKEY SEE CAPER

Thus begins the saga—honey and thumbs, a comedy of lugubrious tubas. How to stay the scald of a saddle? A couple of belts at Winky's—that gamut, a passion. A good, deep dip at the fountain below our fjord. Barbecue jar and butter bucket answered your prayers? Aren't all the girls pretty down here in Kansas City? And see therein lies the rub, Bub—not all Middling-Western card-sharps look one another in the droopy eye when they lift a collective glass of simultaneous congratulations—but it's nice to kiss both cheeks each time we meet on the street full of overly humble trombones and cornet corn playing flats sharply at half staff. That, friends, is tops in axing. Not bad, what? Why the life-chops of the wife of a horse-shoe-tosser, she will surely hurl a ringer once again as seen in the next and final issue of the scrap book saved from heap-night.

FACT AND FANCY

Boy oh boy! Like as a garden of Italian laughter, like as the morning after, like as mead what clogs the arteries—one swift swig and bedtime cometh, an anxious, skittering dervish among the swaying silly. Once we swam along in cool draughts of water unbeknownst but now-a-doldrums. (There is always dust between the slats.) No vacuum is strong enough for the sloth with hair between his toes. No broom is brisk enough for these. Only transplants sing like contra-tenors who recognize a teasing song or whirling dance among our good-fat hours. These locals are hopeless—never so sick, like seasick, like fresh fish from Bushwick sick. The name rhymes. The minute reeks. This is not an argument for the skin of things but rocks of age, easy to blow from their firmament roots. For as any regular reader knows, we'll take the ancient warrior, the full-sized fuselage of that great old favorite of reconnaissance and photography pilots worldwide, an ultra-turbo-sonic-monster-machine. Having never used one of these newfangled contraptions ourselves (or seen one perform its feat of miraculous daring-do) we had to find out just what they did offer his majesty's moustaches. Some weight was needed at the tail to get a flatter glide, but that was all. We could portamento over the globe's new latitudes, smoothly, soothing and slow.

UNCONVINCED VOLCANOLOGIST

All aboard for contribution to the spores of our circumnavigation. We don our helmets steadfast and only doff our helmets forward to the ladies we go to war for, like water caught in a window jamb, like sands in a baby's beach bucket, like smiling ferry-boat captains in overalls. How would everybody like to take a little side-trip to that patch of acne called an archipelago? Good! Hop on! Here where everything's eruptive, adaptive, and brackish and the cough is full of lava from our very deepest of calderas. This beast of truth and its brutal spewing. Forsooth, that lump of an island, that pimple's expulsion, complete with phlegm and all the peace of a fleet of demons. What succor contained in these secretions? None. Here's frenzy in the sea, the difference between whalebacks and white water. A small wave dies and looks like a drowning.

NEAR CHURCHES

If you want to extend the same buying privilege to other members in your fraternal, industrial, social or other group, just fill in and mail this handy postage paid self addressed card. The enclosed is for you and your family and is not transferable. Liberal credit accommodations can be arranged through Baltimore. Your low price remains the same for cash or credit. Maryland, oh my Maryland, what pincers are your kisses now! One can hope. One can dream. One can consume one's portions. One can furthermore hurl invective. Also geology is hard about the head and face. One cannot always keep pace with the scatter hoarders. Their poor throats are parched and thirsty sure from advance applauses! The needle was free on the grooves. So don't be squeamish on the pour! Look at the peanut pocket in their worsted waistcoat's proper-handed drumlin clump of a vestment—full of nuts! Collect them all with gusto and gumption. Best is that man who has found his work and given his message to Garcia. Blessed is that man who doth give his impeccably urgent answer back to the messenger. What fell off the truck? Just a box of watches fell today. Ask Monsignor Cipollone out of Cedarburg, where beige Oldsmobiles hover in abeyance under mustard awnings, where carports are friendly, well-lit and filtered with green plastic-wares over the windows, several shelves of boxes full of numbskull plumbing parts. Under a box is where they hid their findings. Carefully and with precision and consistency they bury their thirty nine findings. They come from the conservatory with their tri-color pencils and their winning grins. They come from the ivy and have small teeth for adult examples.

GROCERY FOOT JOY

Iron City gentlemen, we are in receipt of your telegram of yesterday canceling order for pick eyes, swift. Have you decided to allow us to send you a sample case of the remnants of laces, flounces, tuckers and trimmings? Strictly cash at our regular sugar department and the ladies of the Akron Baptist Home could wish no less for you than to sell you Union metallic bread boards and metal bone novelties. We are in receipt of your order for rolling pins and same shall go forward at once by parcel post. We sell bulk flour at bargain rates. We regret to learn of mines closing down as this makes for a dire outlook for lucrative business in your district. We had most all of the eyes packed and ready for shipment, and they would have gone forward today. We are glad to assign you additional territory as fast as you can use it. And regarding your letter of recent, mostly cloudy date, we beg to advise that we cannot furnish imitation blue grey fox fifty or sixty inches long. Instead, please find enclosed samples of cloth used to make *our* cape. It is a beautiful garment at a low price. Most finally, we have not received your check for the invoice of April 6th to Milton by way of our Biltmore Street store and April 8th to Altoona via the mid-day Cuba Libra local out of Wortheimer. And the small invoice covering 1000 Entertainer Bouquets shipped to Rothermel from late April is also open (you know what they say about cruelty). We are prompted in mentioning this to you because of your unbroken custom of remitting in strict accordance with the ten day terms and it therefore occurs to us that there is a possibility of this last mail having been lost in transit and that being the case you would wish to know it (having left on the 4:00 bus). Oblige, fast freight, god speed. Adding regards, we feel sure that you will accept this letter in the spirit in which it is written and not consider it any form of a dun.

THRIFTY DISPATCH

Plans were unveiled Wednesday night to arrest a 70-year-old Wyoming man in the vicinity of the City of Pewaukee. Cited on suspicion of operating a vehicle while intoxicated, police found the man lying outside his rolled-over car Tuesday night. The man had previously been incarcerated for releasing downspout and sump pump discharge onto neighboring properties. He (furthermore) faces a felony battery charge after attacking a man who had smothered his cockatiel with hair tonic after allegedly drinking pure grain alcohol with some friends Thanksgiving night and into Friday morning's dawn according to a criminal complaint filed Monday in Circuit Court. The suspect had been drinking the special alcohol with his closest friends and others in the victim's house when the former allegedly found his cockatiel covered in a type of goo they soon learned was hair unguent, the complaint shows. The cockatiel later died and the perpetrator allegedly attacked the person presumed responsible for the bird's death. The alleged victim suffered a deep-seated cut to his left eyebrow, a medium-length gash on his upper left torso, extensive blood loss, a bone chip in his wrist and a swollen right ear, the complaint filed four days later shows. The Wyoming man is charged with substantial battery intending bodily harm and faces a maximum term of three years and six months in prison at Mukwonago County, where the fiasco of assaults occurred.

ON PIANO MOUNTAIN

Will this army nurse change your dishwashing habits? Watch as she shows you how her tableware is molded from spruce pulp and is so low priced you might buy small sets for all your houses! Sing it loud and sing on high for truck-sides! How much brown bread, Braunschweig pâté and gherkins can a man, after all, eat? She'll show you how now. She'll let you know when the doctor has discharged. When the bullet is removed. When the stitches are tied up tight. (We do have Spanish fleets galore, Denmark's finest models—all planked hull kits, mahogany and hardwood, fittings of turned brass, including the Bluenose, the Dragon, as well as Shadow yachts and our signature Norwegian Lion, full pictorial replicas of the entire line of the Luftwaffe and a Flemish Galleon to make your nose bleed freely.) When the laundry stops snarling in the wicked wind and the marketplace falters and finally falls, when the small school's holes are bolstered and the hickory stops flickering, when the truck comes from Sweets Corner, when the truck from Whitcomb Summit comes, when the Savoy Mountain truck comes we retire.

DEMENTIA PUGILISTICA

The ex-champion has earned his lesson—last November, a strong and lithely conditioned Ortiz, at 135½ pounds, stepped onto the canvas at Coco, Puerto Rico, for his rematch with the 133-pound Laguna, the latter succumbing in a unanimous decision after fifteen rounds. He learned by guessing. He recalled the time in Toledo, Oregon, as two young men reported their car stolen out from underneath them at Cape Perpetual. The vehicle had a Ford V8 engine with Edelbrock lifters and exhaust headers, La Salle grille, Studebaker headlight rims, a Pontiac bumper, a Dodge hood and a Buick Roadmaster hood ornament. It had 24% more road horsepower—for passing! The men added little else, laughing with the captain at the local headquarters. They were from over by Wallow County and were asked the question by a newspaperman *how do you account for the preponderance of Negro fighters today?* Years ago nearly every fighter was Irish. Now Kid Chocolate, the Cuban Bon-Bon reigns. And so always the smaller city surprises—like grackle spasms in Tarrytown (several thousand grackles). Sooner due—a list of new roses for Tuesday. Also due—a proposal for practical applications at the Center for Loss and Renewal. Sing jolly flatboat men sing out! Don't forget your ten o'clock with the secretary from sales. She's a looker in all three pieces. Something about adjusting her heels. She reflects very nicely from the bus window. See page 43. He withstands a small critique of his layout for the Illustration of a Weighted Checklist Developed on Bake Shop Managers and sometimes he wishes he was just a baker.

LONGEST NAME (ON THE COMICS PAGE)

Wolfeschlegelsteinhausenbergerdorffvoralternwarengewissenhafschaferswessenschafewarrenwohlgepflegundschafwarrenwohlgepflegundsorgfaltigkeitbeschutzenvonangreifendurchihrraubgierigfeindewelchevoralternzwolftausendjahresvoranddieerscheinenvandererersteerdemenschderraumschiffgebrauchlichtalsseinursprungvonkraftgestartseinlangefahrthinzwischensternartigraumaufdersuchenachdiesternwelchegehabtbewohnbaker—But long last names generally need one or two syllable first names. And for charity's sake, it's best not to use a first name that ends with the same sane sound that starts the last name. Gus Snead sounds like flatulence, for example. Yes, choose a name with palimpsest care (most of what he writes he will erase). Don't make his name sound like lawn furniture or hers like a cheap, dime store perfume—Ward Wiesenthal or Myra Wattles for instance. We hope this tip from our modern name book will help you arrange the perfect nomenclature for your spawn. The names for boys follow herewith and the names for girls start on page 14—Aaron is exalted. Basil is a kingly ruler. Cavanaugh, of course, is cavalier. Dale of the Saxon valley. Elmer hales nobility. Fabian's a better farmer. Griswold is of the forest fair. For Herschel see Henry. Hubert, the substitute, is a quicker thinker—nude and starving in the trees (next to Griswold) his stag comes cross-impaled and skull-holed. Iago is a charming bitch. Jervis, they tell us, is belligerent, so don't, in Almighty's baby manual, name your poor son Jervis. Knute of the hill. Lester bright and glorious. Mortimer's a Norman name. Nathan is the gift of god, but if they don't have anything better sometimes, a name's just a gift of god. Orville is a golden city. P names are dull, but Phelan stands for wall-like. If Q is your preference, wait for Quentin, fifth born, or Quincy, also fifth, but the only boy. Tricky, but fun! Reuben, behold a son! Scott is tattooed. Thayer's like a hunting dog. Upton another hill dweller. Vernon will flourish, so will Virgil. Woodrow another white forester. Xavier is sole and famous. Yule will dwell at gates. And our funniest boy, near onomatopoetic, is Zigmond, the winner.

FIVE ACT PLAY WITH EIGHT TABLEUAX

Brilliantine dealers everywhere—do you *hide* the things you value? Sometimes, as you dash away to catch the last train for the theatre, do you furtively stash your valuables in the vase on the library table—behind a picture—underneath the carpet—in a drawer of your chiffonier—under the toilet—in the condiment basket used rarely for picnics? When the things you value are in a fire-proof, knife-proof and ex-husband-locked box you live in the leisurely days of old lavender and stately manners. You are cool as the proverbial tuber. By way of a coiffure ornament there is a bandeau of beautifully cut jet beads with an aigrette rising gracefully from the center front. What women wear in the sketch between acts and tableaux? White satin frocks with slashed sleeves and black panels, representing highlights, like waist decorations. A high girdle of seed pearls with a stiff cluster of black quills sprouting up. And when you want just a few puffs of fine Havana slide out serenely in between any of the acts or tableaux. This fire notice brought to you by the silk hosiery that wears ultra-sheer but not shiny. For three score years and ten—an infinite delicacy, a rare distinction, replete with court beauties in luxurious garden worlds between all five acts and each of the eight tableaux. Sheen free at last are we! This leaflet answers any questions. Send for it to find out.

COMBO PLATTER

Good reading and good snacking fit like fingers in the right bowling ball. How Snappy Cheese fits crackers! It's all cheese and marigolden among the falling-leaf-brown-orange-piles with just a gentle bite and you too can know how it spreads on so very, very SMOOTH. Football! Don't just hint to your wife to bring home Snappy, demand it! America's most distinctive native cheese, meltable, spreadable, sliceable—say Snappy cheese and say it often. Custom blended for mildness. Next to your two shallow bowls of pebbles keep jars of Latakia and Perique, Kentucky Burley and Virginia Bright. Also presently on sale—Carolina Buttery Flake. And now for an amazing milk discovery! Try our favorite Midnight Fish Bait Soup. Just what the ambulance driver ordered for the later evening cure for too much fun with the gents from accounts payable. Just add oleo and powdered milk. Also excellent with a main dish of casseroles, soufflés, flambés or mock chicken legs fully baked. Never, ever filling, even accompanying steaks with a special friend. For starters *and* finishers, make it Snappy.

PAMPHLET ON EMBOSSED ANAGRAMS

In the coal car with coffee boiling, by way of the risen word, a man's world, shiny wood, smoke, pretzels, good conversation and, most of all, six generations of great premium Blatz beer cases. Adventurous, treacherous, precious foodstuffs containing hopscotch and boxcars boxcars boxcars, if you can dig. We fly polar projected. It's a last will and testament paper airplane! Horse-shoeing promptly attended to—*just so* as mother used to say. Ask at your local globetrotter. Ask your cabby. Ask Mr. Ree, soft and thirsty. Ask the Moving Planet Space Game. (Prices higher west of the Mississippi and Canada.) Ask Mississippi and Canada. See if there's a map from Yukon to Tallulah. For half-time snacks serve pizza boats and the new trick with frankfurters. And for the finest in "company" food—prepare thirty nine devilled ham turnovers the night before. Just pop in the oven for a healthful and heartwarming tide-me-over for the armchair quarterback in *your* recliner. Devilled ham turnovers? Just the *best* for your king in an Italian sweater-shirt, for that free and easy feeling. More food for hollow legs. Throat hot? Throat raw? Well something sensational has happened in smoking!

THE BOTTOM DRAWER DRAWINGS

This sheet shows a house broken apart and Holland men have simply got to heat the house. Ask Larry if he's married, hang the fire pot and ease up the ash pit grate. Every heavy Holland's made of core in our Michigan Mother Ship and sent direct from the processing plant in Alpha, Ohio. From Cedar Rapids to Bethlehem we carve basements neat of heat. (And a basement is the heart of a home.) The furnace is the drum kit (of tropical traffic fire) to your family's brassy outfit. You know what's hidden behind that door—bridge drawings in pencil, precarious empty antique boxes in a stack atop the wonky chifforobe, tenuous empty valises in a stack, gargantuan mounds of dispatch cases in (relatively) orderly piles, and binders filled with architectural graph papers barely strewn on stationary stationery from the secretary's secretary. Also remnants of an iron filing magnate's top three desk shelves in a satchel. Holland Men have helped your disinterment and Finland Men have kept the water running. Scotland Men have stacked the papers in a fashion befit for the faint of sight and Poland strode up on horses. Warm up before the storm. Gather your hoarfrost into a snowball.

BORNEO WILD MAN

Women of impulse! Men of violence! Here's another impromptu illusion that can readily be turned into a mystery wrapped with foils of butter-mint-yellow and plastic frill. Follow how—you state that you have a Borneo Wild Man kindly confined in the next room and that perhaps you can persuade him to come out and meet people in one of his gentler moods. But hardly have you gone through the remaining door before you come reeling out again, half-mad, with the Wild Man's hand clawing at your face and his brawny bare arm strangling you by your tensile-puny neck-muscles. After being hauled into the other room, un-obligingly, you finally emerge, saying that people who want to see the Borneo Wild Man can go in there themselves. *Now for review, gather round and let's discuss what we've picked up thus far. Let's take it from what to do if the intruder comes after you. We go to the drawer with the largest knife and what do we do? Stab him? Not quite—rather we stab him repeatedly. Exactly! Now what do we do next? What do we do just in case he comes back at us with snarling resolve? Bite him! Yes, indeed, we bite him with all our might is right!*

POWER OF ATTORNEY TELEGRAM

Glorious Ford amid Eastern Airlines & the swindle of Science Hall butt-up with State Space Park across from Underground World Home, the late model Chrysler, Hertz & Heliport Greyhound Auto Thrill Show, Maritime Union Park, U.S. Rubber & Terrible Transportation & Cumbersome Travel Pavilion Industry. Take Idaho Lowenbrau Garden Tour of Dinosaur World & Hawaiian Carnival—for champagne flying on a beer budget. Check Florida Water-ski Show Amphitheatre. Check Florida Boat Ride & Live Porpoise Dolphin and Tuna Show on Continental Park Memorial Memorabilia Monorail through perfect little Carousel Carousing Park, Chung King Roadway Inn at Walter's International Wax Museum featuring Les Poupeés de Paris. Green flies big as Chattanooga Buicks. At last relax over dancing aerial waters taking Jaycopters & Flume Rides all of this & more for you only with redeemable coupon for three cartons of French's Parakeet Biscuit with vitamin B-12 for a less rigorous dander, French's, the vigor-building biscuit. Mail coupon today & receive our all-new 39 page catalogue offering cuttle bone, treat & gravel & fool-proof lessons on how to train your pet to talk & do tricks! Remit to Mustard Street General Post, Rochester 9, New York. So another sawbuck on bitter beer for the cafeteria-style-research chaps again because all a young child needs for this hobby are murder net, killing jar, corrugated cardboard for incarceration containers, tweezers or pinning forceps, paper strips, liquid cement, pins, cotton for spreading & cleaning & cigar box for preserving your fourth-born child's enduring legacy of unlimited & animatedly, decidedly rare & scarce trove of unexpected treasures.

SOUVENIR

As the stationmaster (maestro of the flower-beds) snacked on his unusually uneventful and leisurely vinegar crisp, pedestrian beet juice and briefly steeped pennyroyal with milk and a half-spoon of honey, three burly workmen opened the lately arrived luggage hatch doors with a flourish and (hence) a sequence of empty coffins were cautiously paired with their tombstones (since lost). Therein was (regardless) a feast of death for sure in this delivery. These inside long dead, indeed, entire. Preserved in belated glass and then non-fugitive plastic, boxed well and quite properly for their value and their worth, there will be no update on their progress. A stationmaster aghast and a public (emphatic) will pay just enough attention. We murmured. *Whence came they?* We said. *You can't change the weather, but you can forecast it.* When the water drops, batten the hatches. And no photography please. And still they snap away at the empty caskets.

MORE FUN IN THE WATER

We interrupt this program to bring you lightweight, homemade gear for explorer adventurers. Note these super features—double shoulders, action armholes, extended knee patches, bias-cut fronts, reinforced stitching, gripper closings and belt pants for that long-lasting feeling of comfort, ease, ingenuity and durability. Of course he wears most of these things simultaneously, but he does have extra sox and an extra pair of under-drawers. Consistency's own hobgoblin, a pancake without syrup, a donut with no girl. His sweat shirt serves as both pajama top and jacket. Sing him soup songs and go bowling for dollars. He made his own buckskin camp moccasin. If he turns over the visor-cap you might observe that the underside of the brim has a pair of flip-down sun glasses clipped to it. And for food, ah, now we're getting somewhere. Notice our friend carries mostly dry stuffs. Keep it light but right. He'll camp near good water—so why carry it with him? Each meal is in its own distinctively colored bag. His forethought is rare as the blessed strike right after the cursed spare. And for more fun in the water, mix peanuts and whisky on eight great factory tours. You don't have to be a swimmer to compete. The soggy guy bringing up the long rear in this (old home week) wheelbarrow race looks waterlogged—even if he's only waist deep in the murky mud. Just pick a buddy who looks like a winner, and wheel him away. Sing him soup songs for marbles and bocce balls. As you grow older, after all, peanuts and whisky mix on eight great factory tours quite nicely. While we swing into abstraction, better whoop and why not relax and have another sandwich. Brush up on your triplicate tractate and always remember Ravenna even when you're in Vancouver. Speed never slumps. He is eagle. You are poor. Better buy two copies of the swan song now for your needle will grind this platter down to a veritable membrane. Keep up the good splashing and afterwards there's archery!

WENT TO MEXICO

Seems like it's all going to be okay after all. We inhabit Oklahoma with what once was our grimace and is now a grin (from back home in Manhattan). Somebody needs a new helmet. He is the burly ventricle and atrium refurbisher and she is operator of the heart crane, and one more thing—her toes are small tomatoes. (And just as delectable to the tongue and tan to touch.) She allows one to put his own shell up to her ear to hear the anguished sobs of her long-remembered seascape now near-forgot for the jungle in her smirk of trees during the Royal Mail Steam Packet Company's saloon breakfast at Orduña (off Orizaba)—the compote of prunes, oats and flakes and wheats with cream, bluefish, kippered herrings, minced collops, brain fritters, three eggs turned, kidneys a la Diable, roast mutton, corned pork, semolina cakes, imperial of egg salad and consommé Jardinière, ox tongue Florentine, runner beans, cheeses and biscuits and profiteroles, celery Remolade, shrimp with pickles and peas, hot perogi of mushroom, meat or cabbage, four kinds of nuts & occidental sweets, Rowanberry liqueurs and you can tick off your gins and check your pinch-points. If you're a whisky-drinker also find a tick-sheet next to the peanut salver. If you're a Scotch man, top notch! At the fantail is featured just after last call for breakfast dishes, a death this noon off the steamer, with fellowship over, white suit pressed right, death at noon (and how) but love is many splintered at the splay and the splash anyway, tower roomful or no. Rough trick or suicide, nevertheless, dead.

SILKY DUCK

Our steadfast subject paused for what seemed an insufferable instant. Men do not usually eat so well without women. In between the green dish of voodoo and the golden dish of Hindu stood his answer—jelly. He could see in his lady friend's porphyry eyes that he had done well done with his collection of spoons and creams. Perhaps next time with a parsnip daub for the first palate. Yes. What seemed like such a short time ago he was known by few and understood by none. But now her arrow had found its mark. The reality was he could not sleep with the thought of the breast and thigh meat going into the stew. The sturdy Aurora bowl and the hard Cincinnati chargers of royal and white likewise shone. Roar across this clearing house country. Roll along in song. He's heard stories of folks who don't believe in oxymoronic-good Winnipeg bacon. Long live the king, Cincinnatus. Don your apron, sodden gents, fragrant, abiding, and plangent, just add meat.

FROM THE BUREAU OF THREATS AND OPPORTUNITIES

Wishes are catacombs—built for loss and stain-fast, they crumble overnight (of a sudden). So he lands on Yulee by the border at last. He clutches his temples not without drama, but it feels good. The children are outside screaming, sometimes *fire* and sometimes *liar* and sometimes *fire* and *liar* at the same time. Not his children. There's a long haired man eating a mango on the avenue—six weeks in the clean white clink. (He wishes he was Dutch again and then regrets it.) How about that for cadenza embellishment? This will be his summer of white horses. Even in the city, six white horses. Life is rough on the streets of the city and life is soft in the circles of the suburbs. Real men wear belts. If he's dead he won't smell her towel again. She would be sole executrix of the proving of 700 dollars, the falcon's yellow ass-feathers and a Fantasia for Keyboard with forty hands, also featuring melodic flourish.

THE DEATHBED VERSION

Local Boy Finds Rhyme with *Orange—Door-hinge!* Loses Fight for Life in Hospital. As we go to press—last minute news from East to West—Canadian student kills the infamous trickster, who, with his company cronies went to Schenectady by car. These were among his final freedoms. At Schenectady in synecdoche, he clanked the planks. His removal from the hotel to the hospital was made at the suggestion of the manacles and high wires. Our mystifier braved death by the blows of a strong Montreal student who was stupid according to accounts of several eye witnesses. Crossing the northern border was our hero's demise, his nemesis. But no man-made device could keep him bound. Only the audit of a young Quebecois man's fisticuffs, god-given killers of the American favorite, afforded the interruption and, ultimately, the final autopsy. A quick succession of blows burst his belly. He died from poison in the widening gyre and the un-wobbling pivot. He died with suspicious hair for our times. For his times that coif was Algerian in the Wisconsin dust. Only colors don't rhyme. And eagle and owl together, then, dismember him. He is survived by our Holy Mother of the Pregnant Pause, who understands that art is long but not always why a headstone need be so costly. Four roses, white roses and cash donations will be handled Thursday at the Elks Club on Whiterock Avenue where it intersects with Arcadian at dusk, sharp. A memorial service remains to be announced. We still need an echo for silver and a proper word to balance purple.

THE SLEEP OF OMBUDSMEN

By order of neon magnitude, a heap of tweed jacket elbows on the library leather, artfully categorized articles of an evangelical elegy for the whole deck's fifty-two proverbs brought back in time, the clockwork's wicked Egyptian subtractions, a crooked clock, a broken clock, rubber galoshes and a cloak-pile, a corridor full of basketball action snapshots, a chronicle of the bitter beyond in twelve other volumes, a pitiless voice from the hinterland, flap-copy memory of an urban amateur meteorologist and shutter-bug caught in pirouette between two city blocks, horoscope and hourglass. Each speck trickles, the strumpet within the strumpet within the steam table over the lower-middle-western side of town. Here's the belly where we burgeon. The late day of this year was a deeply deflated purple kick-ball in a playground littered by kick-balls about to pop. We don't know what we mean. We take a taxi to the office in our short-pants stained blue and brown on purpose. Come quick to see the Über-Italian fanfares and Antique Greek overtures and Holy German animadversions, the sinking inklings with incremental inflections. The Frenchman is deaf and smells of pepper. The railroad commissioners chatter around the snooker-pool-table while children reach our roadhouse hide-away, raucous. Hand the glass over, half-full. Dusk was a slightly deflated Oldsmobile wheelhouse casing with a copy of the Picayune in the back window, accepting the sunshine's dying grip. One more before we bid our quilt the endless graces. One before we shine. Smell the fear, like brisket sweat. One for the horrible, heralded road. One more before we fold.

MAP OF THE 1965 WORLD'S FAIR
QUEENS, NEW YORK

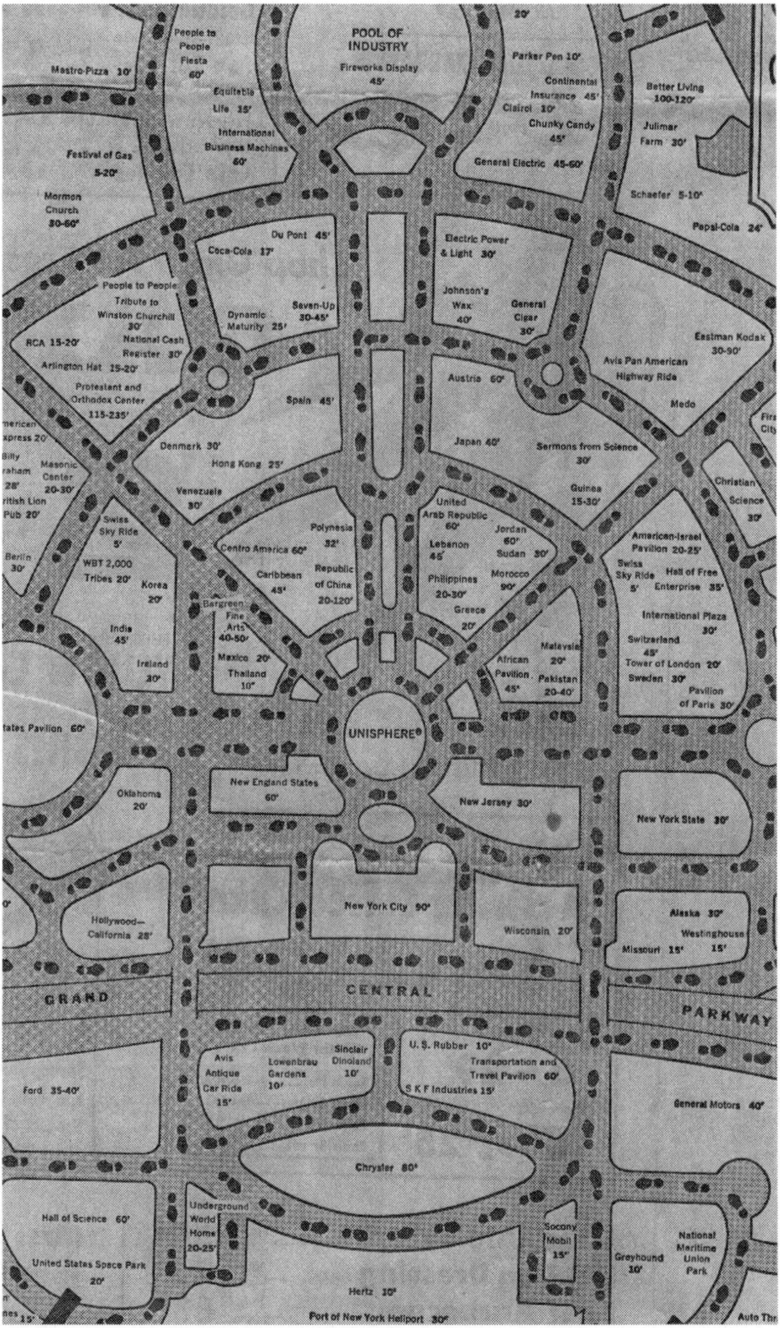
POOL OF INDUSTRY
Fireworks Display 45'
People to People Fiesta 60'
Mastro-Pizza 10'
Equitable Life 15'
International Business Machines 60'
Parker Pen 10'
Continental Insurance 45'
Clairol 10'
Chunky Candy 45'
General Electric 45-60'
Better Living 100-120'
Julimar Farm 30'
Schaefer 5-10'
Pepsi-Cola 24'
Festival of Gas 5-20'
Mormon Church 30-60'
Du Pont 45'
Coca-Cola 17'
Electric Power & Light 30'
Johnson's Wax 40'
General Cigar 30'
People to People Tribute to Winston Churchill 30'
RCA 15-20'
National Cash Register 30'
Arlington Hat 15-20'
Dynamic Maturity 25'
Seven-Up 30-45'
Eastman Kodak 30-90'
Avis Pan American Highway Ride
Medo
Protestant and Orthodox Center 115-235'
Spain 45'
Austria 60'
Denmark 30'
Hong Kong 25'
Japan 40'
Sermons from Science 30'
Venezuela 30'
Guinea 15-30'
Christian Science 30'
Masonic Center 20-30'
Swiss Sky Ride 5'
Polynesia 32'
Centro America 60'
United Arab Republic 60'
Jordan 60'
Lebanon 45'
Sudan 30'
American-Israel Pavilion 20-25'
Berlin 30'
WBT 2,000 Tribes 20'
Korea 20'
Caribbean 45'
Republic of China 20-120'
Philippines 20-30'
Morocco 90'
Swiss Sky Ride 5'
Hall of Free Enterprise 35'
Greece 20'
International Plaza 30'
India 45'
Bergreen Fine Arts 40-50'
Mexico 20'
Thailand 10'
Ireland 30'
Malaysia 20'
African Pavilion 45'
Pakistan 20-40'
Switzerland 45'
Tower of London 20'
Sweden 30'
Pavilion of Paris 30'
UNISPHERE®
New England States 60'
Oklahoma 20'
New Jersey 30'
New York State 30'
New York City 90'
Hollywood— California 25'
Wisconsin 20'
Alaska 30'
Westinghouse 15'
Missouri 15'
GRAND
CENTRAL
PARKWAY
Avis Antique Car Ride 15'
Lowenbrau Gardens 10'
Sinclair Dinoland 10'
U. S. Rubber 10'
Transportation and Travel Pavilion 60'
S K F Industries 15'
Ford 35-40'
General Motors 40'
Chrysler 60'
Hall of Science 60'
Underground World Home 20-25'
Socony Mobil 15'
Greyhound 10'
National Maritime Union Park
United States Space Park 20'
Hertz 10'
Port of New York Heliport 30'

NOTES to the SECTIONS

FIRST DRAFT OF A PREFACE Macaronicon (a macaronic medley of languages). Naz-Dar (Chicago) *Stencil Unit Reproduction Information* (n/d).

SECOND DRAFT OF A PREFACE Jack Sharkey—born 1902, Heavyweight Champion, 1928-30, 1932-33.

THIRD DRAFT OF A PREFACE Kress & Co. Retail Price List, for Bodmer's Old Reliable Bolting Cloth (nd) 372 Gold Street, Brooklyn. Meine kleine Bahnhofhallenbüchlein. "My little penny dreadful," Tom Whalen's *Written on a Whim,* of Robert Walser's *Speaking to the Rose, Bookforum* February 2006. Aktendeckelkarton - cardboard dossier cover. Mayakovsky, Shamberk, Nabokov.

PASSION WAXES was written in Chicago in March 2004.

INDIANAPOLIS THE METROPLOIS is for Joe Smith.

CHICAGO LOUSY WITH POETS is for Bryan Tomasovich and was written in Chicago in March 2004.

COLUMNS BY A CALM POOL *The Blum Family History,* H.E. Blum—*A History of Manitowoc County,* Ralph G. Plumb; Dr. Louis Falge and testimony from parishioners.

PROPOSAL FOR A FOURTH AVENUE KIOSK Kid Chocolate is The Cuban Bon Bon.

CALIFORNIA WELCOMES YOU! the title is from a drawing by Harold Ansley. Also text from *California Limited* brochure, 1920's. In the early 1960s film-maker Hollis Frampton lived in New York spending a nineteen month period at 13 different addresses.

A GLORY OF MAUDLIN WATER the first draft of this was written in New Orleans in February 1994.

THE DIAPER PEOPLE *Household Magazine,* October 1956.

THE STONING OF DUMSHOWMEN is for David Weast and Ward Wiesenthal.

GRAMMATICA IOWA is for Joe Klapper, 1930 Parkers Brothers pamphlet *Battle Game of Knights and Men.*

AUTHORIZATION TO DESTROY INVENTORY Wordsworth's *Prelude, Boring Postcards, Woman's Day,* July 1954.

THE WRECK OF BIG VALLEY is for Gary Edwards and Tim Clark.

MONKEY SEE CAPER *Kansas City Confidential* (1952).

FACT AND FANCY *Flying Models* magazine (n/d).

UNCONVINCED VOLCANOLOGIST was written in Ecuador in January 2005.

NEAR CHURCHES is for Nick Cipollone, who also provided the author with the cover image in Milwaukee circa 1989. Title from Nabokov.

THRIFTY DISPATCH is for Ernest Loesser, after the fact.

ON PIANO MOUNTAIN was written in North Adams, Massachusetts in Spring 2005.

DEMENTIA PUGLISTICA 1965 *Mechanics Illustrated* cartoon. Jimmy Jemail's *The Inquiring Fotographer* (nd)

LONGEST NAME (ON THE COMIC PAGE) Mennen *Baby Manual* (nd) Philip H. Love, *(Washington) Evening Star,* (article abruptly torn off at "wohnba") (found—estate sale, Chevy Chase, Maryland).

FIVE ACT PLAY WITH EIGHT TABLEAU Cora Mann Times Square Theater Program October 1921.

PAMPHLET ON EMBOSSED ANAGRAMS *Popular Science,* 1957, *Woman's Day,* 1954, Selchow and Righter Company, New York.

THE BOTTOM DRAWER DRAWINGS 1926 Holland (Michigan) Furnace Company brochure. 1928 Leedy (Indianapolis) Drummer's Instruments Catalog R.

POWER OF ATTORNEY TELEPGRAPH *Woman's Day* July 1954.

SOUVENIR is for Kent Mueller.

MORE FUN IN THE WATER Boy's Life *Litepac Camping Equipment,* Boy's Life *Swimming and Waterfront Activities* 1956.

SILKY DUCK Penzey's Spice Catalog *Creative Cook's Corner* also Lucius Quinctius Cincinnatus.

SLEEP OF OMBUNDSMEN (152) proverbs, Benjamin Peret and Paul Éluard, 1924, Billing Boats advertisement, *Flying Models,* November (n/d).

Sections of *IMPATIENCE* appeared elsewhere as follows—

CERTIFICATE OF AUTHENTICITY
appeared in *DIAGRAM*, Issue 5.2, Spring 2005.

HANGOVER CURE FOR MEN
UNCONVINCED VOLCANOLOGIST
appeared in *The Emergency Almanac,* Volume 5, Summer 2005.

CALIFORNIA WELCOMES YOU!
GRAMMATICA IOWA
HANGOVER CURE FOR MEN
THE STONING OF DUMBSHOWMEN
appeared in *KNOCK* #9, Spring 2007.

DRAFT OF A PREFACE #1
DRAFT OF A PREFACE #2
DRAFT OF A PREFACE #3
appeared in *The Siennese Shredder*, Volume #2, 2007.

WINTRY LODGE ON A WHITE MOUNTAIN
FROM THE BUREAU OF THREATS AND OPPORTUNITIES
appeared in the *Iowa Review,* Volume 39, Number 3, Spring 2009.

THE DEATHBED VERSION
appeared in *The Believer,* Volume 7, Number 7, September 2009.

IMPATIENCE—AN INTERVIEW WITH SCOTT ZIEHER

by Kathleen Eull

KE—*IMPATIENCE* is the second book in a sequence you call *Triskaidekalog*. Can you to talk a little about the origins of the name and how you came to it?

SZ—I'm writing thirteen book-length poems and that's just my way to refer to them all at once. I've worked over the number thirteen since I started writing seriously, printing a half dozen chapbooks of thirteen poems, culminating in a failed attempt to write a 21 line poem a day for an entire year in twelve little gilt pocket ambulance supply company date books with 21 lines per diem, corresponding exactly to the months of 1954 and 1993, the year I attempted it. It would have equaled 28 thirteens with a single coda and it was a miserable failure. I abandoned it when I entered my MFA at Columbia. The thirteen fascination ultimately relates to the date of my father's death, Friday, August 13th, 1965. It's not morbid to me, but a number that relates to rebirth. So this "triskaidekalog" is the terminus of that conception, being thirteen book-length poems. Thirteen has always been a manageable number for me—metrics, line count, consecutive sequences. This "triskaidekalog" was a thorough-going way to broaden the possibilities. My first book revolved around a list including the number 39, and my father was 39 when he died. *IMPATIENCE* takes that one further and has 52 sections, and also includes the number 65 by way of the maps and list of attractions from the 1965 World's Fair in Queens. It's very loose and esoteric, and ultimately the divisions of thirteen just keep me conceptualizing a way to take a deep breath. I have a general outline and apparatus prepared for all thirteen books and a fair amount of rough material for the third and fourth poems. I've been reading Ron Silliman's *the Alphabet* to gear up for the long haul.

***IMPATIENCE* was built over quite a long period of time. I would think each part must be written with an eye to the whole. Is that the case or was it more organic than that—and where does that first bit come from?**

In fact the bulk of the sections were completed in about two years. I've tinkered with the whole until now. The first four sections were written at a bar and restaurant called Berghoff's on West Adams

Street in Chicago after the first AWP book fair conference with Emergency Press. Those sections essentially remain as they were written that afternoon in late March, 2004. At that particular point, my first book-length poem was finished and would be published in the following year. So *IMPATIENCE* was immediately a sustained sequence, as I was completely dedicated to the idea of writing thirteen book length poems. After returning to New York I continued in this vernacular I'd uncovered at the bar in Chicago. I felt I'd tapped a rich vein of lost language, our vast American printed matter and ephemera—and it seemed limitless. To me every line has an eye to the whole. I felt it should be organic and fast, contained only by the broad blocks of prose, which was completely unfamiliar territory. I do write press releases for the gallery and that played into the conception of *IMPATIENCE*. Here, though, I felt very comfortable adding a string of adjectives to sections whole cloth from *Good Housekeeping* or an ad from a model airplane magazine or instructions from a feed manual for mink farms. It was important to me, though, that chronologically the first sections after the prefaces were the first to be written and the last parts of the book were the last. I tinkered a little with the guts of the poem, but the parts were essentially sequential.

Your book-length poem *VIRGA* (Emergency Press, 2005) has been said to be Whitmanic in voice. *IMPATIENCE* has quite a different feel. The cadence here is equal parts moribund insurance underwriter, slippery ad man and beery carnival barker. In fact, you've described the voice as a "quirky, stolen language." Is this part of your own progression or an occasional voice you've wanted to develop?

A little bit of both. I think the voice is still pretty manic. In the past I had consciously tried hard not to use too many proper nouns. *VIRGA* moved away from that and with *IMPATIENCE*, I wanted to completely give in, completely run off the tracks. Hence the title, in a way—the second book embodies my impatience with that stricture, with the relative lyrical focus of *VIRGA*. *IMPATIENCE* is stolen language, credited as much as possible in the notes. I think all of these books will reckon with Whitman, Pound, Eliot, Crane, Berryman, Olson, Zukofsky and frankly any book length attempt—Robert Kelly, Diane Wakowski, Ashbery, Merrill, Silliman, there's an incredible list of Americans alone preoccupied with the maximal effort. I'm still not finished with the modern era, and still remain pretty comfortable there. It's one of the best ways for me to remain focused on working a poem, concentrating on these past masters. Why else would anyone pay attention?

It is not uncommon for poets to have at least one pivotal or defining experience, something they spend the better part of years trying to write through or around. The most striking example for you is your father who died before you were born. He turns up here in "CERTIFICATE OF AUTHENTICITY." Can you talk about how that absence has shaped you as a poet?

I'm fascinated with the time period he was alive. All of this is really my attempt to invent a father. For that reason it's also decidedly anachronistic and unapologetically male in focus. Much of what I wrote until my mother died in 1999 was written to honor him. Now it's with both of them in mind that I write, but it's my father who walks through these poems. He was a traveling salesman; my mother was the secretary to the principal at my Junior high school and when I was younger she worked at a rest home called the Avalon Manor. She also moonlighted as a bartender at my brother's bowling alley after retiring. My mother fostered my proclivities toward writing very early. She gave me notebooks whenever we would travel and urged me to write down my impressions; it was something her mother always did when she traveled. In effect I've been doing this since 1974. My grandfathers were employed as a milkman and blacksmith at a paper mill. I also have a fetish for old paper and office supplies. It seems logical to me that my fascination with ephemera comes from these immediate forebears—recapturing fragments of their more optimistic time.

The current climate of poetry remains heavy on confessional poetry. A work like *IMPATIENCE* falls well outside this realm, but there are still elements that are internal. How much of your own history gets woven into a piece like this?

Very little, though I must say that I traveled a lot during the time I wrote this poem and some of the locales are a direct result of visits to the places named. They're referred to in the notes section as much as possible. A further restriction for the overall thirteen book approach was to keep the voice New York-centric, so the title plays into that as well—pulling away from New York to make forays or drop hints to the other 49 states and the two protectorates and Canada, however anonymously, or cryptically—able to approach all of America and beyond. I did try very hard to stay away from maps or take the easy route and instead located what I could on my own via leafing through a pretty huge collection of ephemera I've built up.

How do you answer critics who say that this kind of writing is more transcription or translation than poetry?

Would there were critics clamoring at my door. I'd say *try harder.*

Let's talk more about the title *IMPATIENCE.* I immediately thought of the opening of Charles Olson's 1948 essay on Ezra Pound, "GrandPa, GoodBye" (*Collected Prose: Charles Olson*, University of California Press, 1997):

> **"There is a haste in Pound, but it does not seem to be rushing to any future or away from any past." It is mere impatience, the nerves turning like a wild speed-machine (it is how he got his work done) and, more important, an intolerance of the mind's speed (fast as his goes), an intolerance even of himself. For he is not as vain as he acts. '30 yrs, 30 yrs behind the time'—you hear it from him, over and over."**

Pound is one of your influences. You include a passage from his *Guide to Kulchur* as an epigraph. How did you come to Pound's work? Did you have Olson's observations in mind when you chose the title or is it a happy coincidence?

That's a happy coincidence, but I have actually read Pound's "30 years behind the time" rantings. I came to Pound through reading Joyce. Ever since I think I've aspired to those high-modern ideals, Joyce's and Pound's, so yes, 30 years too late I do relate to. But Pound is particularly inspiring because he wrote music and translated and dealt art and cared for artist's estates and spent just as much energy promoting other's art and writing than he did on his own enormous output. So I relate to that as an art dealer. Pound's letters alone dwarf the best of any subsequent poet's entire creative output. Pound's criminal political obsessions aside, he was a prolific polymath and an influential poet, however quaint and marginalized he's become. Only 100 years ago he was bursting at the seams. It's not that long ago. And as regards the title IMPATIENCE, I am generally not very patient.

The three prefaces are very much the poetic equivalent of a thesis statement, laying out your case for this poem as well as your own larger poetics. Explain how they came about last—perhaps as you tried to solidify the scope of the whole project in your own mind?

I felt a need to qualify where this all came from, I essentially wanted to announce this as a follow up to *VIRGA* by way of "a found song" and "a second breath" in the "baker's dozen," and these would be siphoned from the most obscure sources I could get my hands on. So I listed everything I had summoned to summarize.

Twice now you've mentioned breath—earlier referring to "conceptualizing a way to take a deep breath" and just now "second breath"—this sounds like something that is very much a part of your process. Is yours akin to projective verse, to Olson asserting that the line comes from the breath and that it is the secret of a poem's energy?

Olson's pretty ingrained on the American poet's practice. But these lines don't break, so the breath will by design be greatly exaggerated. These are chunks of a screed, and therefore this poem is difficult to read aloud from without either some sarcasm or a fever pitch. Listen to Olson read aloud and there's no special breath working through the performance—more like huffing and puffing. The impatience extends to that as well—I didn't want to fuss over the breath's influence on the line visually, didn't want to mess too much on the page. It started that way in Chicago because I was running out of notebook space. It's a good, sturdy container, the prose block.

Sound is vitally important to each segment of *IMPATIENCE.* You manage a good ear for American regionalism or as you write, "a walking rain of national phrases." How do you listen to a poem as you write?

That's a really great and strange question. I think I listen to a poem by paying attention. This language is always available. I want to pay attention to music, and art and writing of all kinds, including anyone overheard on the New York City street and absolutely as much American poetry as I can take. The regionalism, I suppose comes with a Mid-Western upbringing, and paying attention to that with a crooked eye. "Walking rain" incidentally, is another word for virga, or rain that evaporates before it hits the ground. I've been told that's what they call it in New Mexico anyway. Hunting for rain that evaporates before it hits the ground—it's an apt definition for a poem.

As a gallery owner, visual art plays a central role in your life. Is art a natural outgrowth of your writing or did the love of art come first?

Poetry came first, but I was lucky to have two art history classes in high school, and that was what I studied in college. I was in "college" for nine years and during most of that time I was also lucky to be a weekly regular at the Metropolitan Gallery in Milwaukee—so I was seeing a contemporary art gallery at work from about 1988. I met weekly with the Goal Zero poetry group there. Artists have always been very important to me. And now most of my time is dedicated to the gallery, twenty years later, and it really couldn't be any other way. I've always had to work and find a way to write, and nothing could be more inspiring for a poet than working this closely with artists. I'm also fortunate to have some flexibility in my time when really necessary.

You have a long view and are often working on multiple projects simultaneously, so, what's next?

The third poem in the sequence revolves around Hollywood movies and magazines, specifically *GENTRY,* a gorgeous men's magazine of which I acquired a full run of 22 quarterly issues from 1951-57. I have a book coming out with powerHouse books in Brooklyn that details a group of photographs I found in the garbage on East 16th Street. I also have a manuscript of shorter poems that don't reflect work on the larger project, called *SEE ALSO AMERICANA*. Those poems go back to 1992 and are more lyrical, formal in some cases, and more personal. I'm hoping to help launch a press with my old friend Joe Smith in Milwaukee with the publication of that book sometime in the next year. I'm also getting married, moving the gallery and finding a new apartment, so, generally—welcome upheavals.

Kathleen Eull lives and writes in Waukesha, Wisconsin. Her work has appeared in The Emergency Almanac and KNOCK.

THANKS—

Kathleen Eull
Jason Gitlin
Jayson Iwen
Joe Smith
André Pretorius
Adam Winner

SPECIAL THANKS—

Andrea Smith

SCOTT ZIEHER won the 2004 Emergency Press book contest for his first book *VIRGA*. Centered on a series of snapshots of the 1964-65 World's Fair in New York, *IMPATIENCE* marks the second in a projected series of thirteen book-length poems dedicated to an anachronistic view of America and the lost details of modern life. Zieher was born in Waukesha, Wisconsin and has lived in New York City since 1992. He is co-owner of ZieherSmith, a contemporary art gallery, founded in 2003 and dedicated to the work of emerging artists in all media.

Author portrait by André Pretorius
2009, watercolor on paper

Printed in the U.S.A. by Lightning Source on acid-free, 30% post-consumer content recycled paper.

Emergency Press participates in the Green Press Initiative, a non-profit organization that is, "working to advance the inclusion of environmental and social impacts as additional measures of corporate success. These ecological goals for industry transformation include:

- Responsible Fiber Sourcing in Paper Production through the elimination of book papers with fiber that originates from endangered forests

- Maximizing the Use of Postconsumer Recycled and Alternative Fibers as a means of supporting the continued development of an environmentally superior fiber infrastructure

- Minimizing Consumption as the most effective means of conserving resources

- Preferencing Chlorine Free Products in an effort to support bleaching processes that minimize toxic discharges in our waterways"

BOOKS FROM EMERGENCY PRESS

Ouisconsin: The Dead in Our Clouds, by Bryan Tomasovich
ISBN 0-9753623-0-5, Paperback, $15.00

VIRGA, a Poem by Scott Zieher
ISBN 0-9753623-1-3, Paperback, $15.00

Six Trips in Two Directions, by Jayson Iwen
ISBN 0-9753623-2-1, Paperback, $15.00

The Border Will Be Soon: Meditations on the Other Side, by Chad Faries
ISBN 0-9753623-3-X, Paperback, $15.00

Touched by Lightning, by Ernest Loesser
ISBN 978-0-9753623-4-1, Paperback, $15.00

Emergency Press is the imprint of the Emergency Collective. A New York non-profit organization, the press is also a member and grant recipient of The Council of Literary Magazines and Presses, and a participant in the Green Press Initiative. The collective also publishes a literary arts blog at emergencypress.org/almanac.

Emergency Press
emergencypress.org
press@emergencypress.org